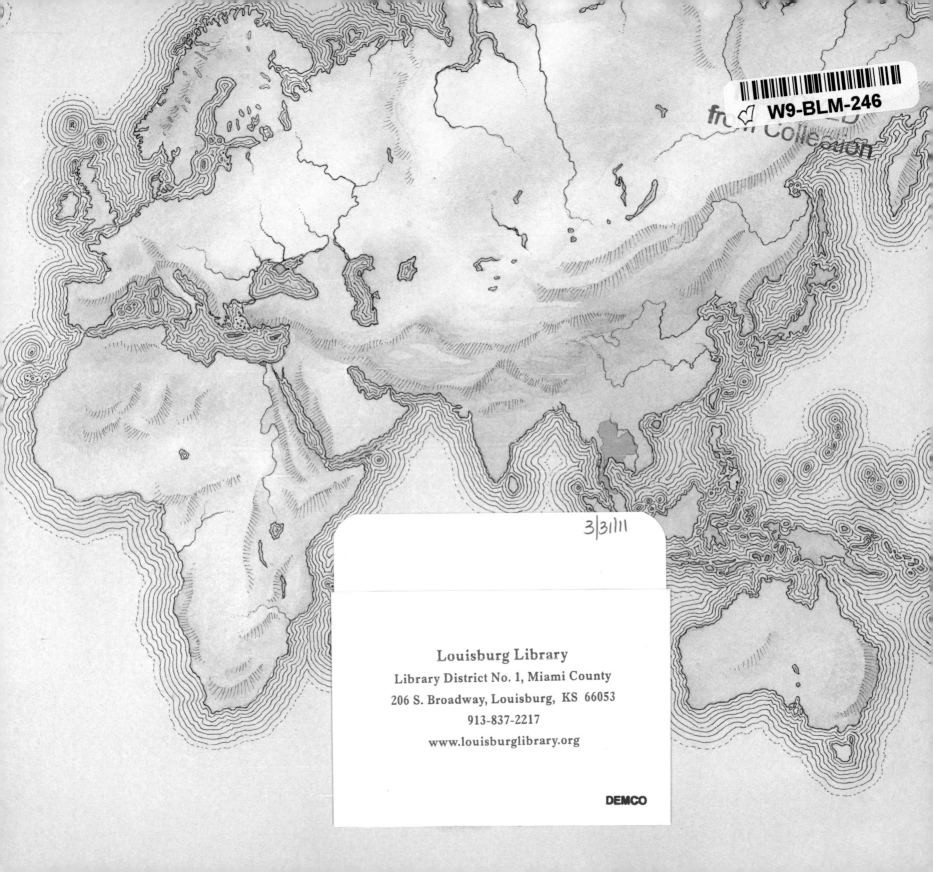

THE LIFE OF RICE

For Daniel — who knows the joys of light in Thai rice fields and continues to explore the flavors every day

Acknowledgments

I am grateful for the support and assistance of friends and colleagues who helped me to complete this book. For their hospitality, insights into the Thai rice culture, and an unforgettable birthday party, I am indebted to my Thai hosts, Colonel Tevannuwat Aniruth Dewa and his wife, Aey. The Tourism Authority of Thailand aided in logistics and introduced me to my guides and translators, Komsan Suwannarat and Noppadon Tempsinpadung. Maria Kuhn and the staff of the Four Seasons Resort in Chiang Mai gave me the unique opportunity to watch rice grow and get harvested right from my balcony. Thanks to Paul Seigel, Jak Severson, Russ Fill, Chris Wicke, and Cosmo, who shared torrential downpours, tropical sun, and frisky primates during my earlier visits to Thailand. Thanks to my agent and friend Susie Cohen and to my patient and insightful editors at Candlewick Press, Kate Fletcher, Karen Lotz, and Maryellen Hanley. As always, Daniel Sobol, Ronne Mae Weiss, and Betty Bardige gave me helpful comments and suggestions to help me mold the story. Chalee Kioechui of the Baan Thai restaurant in Waltham, Massachusetts, helped with the Thai language translations and made me some of his famous sticky rice with mango. Special thanks to the Atlantic Spice Company in Truro, Massachusetts. They keep me stocked with a full assortment of Thai rice while I am home on Cape Cod.

• •

First edition 2010

Library of Congress Cataloging-in-Publication Data
Sobol, Richard.
 The life of rice : from seedling to supper / Richard Sobol. —1st ed.
   p. cm.
 ISBN 978-0-7636-3252-6
1. Rice — Juvenile literature. I. Title.
SB191.R5S635 2010
633.1'809593 — dc22   2009015138

15 14 13 12 11 10
CCP 10 9 8 7 6 5 4 3 2 1

Printed in Shenzhen, Guangdong, China

This book was typeset in Dante and Interstate.

Candlewick Press
99 Dover Street
Somerville, Massachusetts 02144

visit us at www.candlewick.com

THE LIFE OF RICE

>> **From Seedling to Supper** «

RICHARD SOBOL

CANDLEWICK PRESS

MYANMAR
(BURMA)

LAOS

CHIANG MAI

THAILAND

Issan Province

NAKHON
RATCHASIMA • BURI-RAM
• SURIN

BANGKOK

CAMBODIA

VIETNAM

Andaman Sea

Gulf of
Thailand

MALAYSIA

On my first visit to Thailand, I teamed up with special agents from the Thai Wildlife Protection Police force. We sped from province to province, gathering evidence that would be used to protect Thailand's threatened and endangered species. I carried secret pocket cameras and a tiny video lens hidden inside a pair of fake eyeglasses to help identify and capture illegal animal hunters and smugglers.

As the miles passed, I gazed out of helicopter windows and the open roofs of police vans and watched the Thai countryside. Over and over again I saw scenes of enormous rice fields glistening in the warm glow of the tropical light. Although my photo assignment was focused on protecting Thai wildlife, my imagination as a photographer constantly drew me to the textures and pastel colors of Thai farmers engulfed in the waves of their rice.

When I saw a woman ahead in a bright yellow silk shirt frozen in a soft blanket of green rice plants, I couldn't bear it anymore. I asked permission to stop for just one minute, and the Thai police commander, Colonel Dewa, reluctantly agreed. "Make it quick," he said as I grabbed my camera. "I am only letting you do this because for Thai people, rice is what keeps us alive. It is as important to us as the air that we breathe."

I had just enough time for one photograph that day, but I knew then that I had to return. I wanted to photograph and learn more about rice, this single crop that meant so much to the Thai people.

Richard Sobol

My life as a photographer involves a lot of fast-paced travel followed by slower times at home as I review and edit my photographs. One day, while I was working at home, I went outside to check the mail and there, on the top of the mailbox, was a letter unlike any I had ever received before. The envelope was decorated with gold inscriptions and regal seals.

I opened it excitedly, wondering who had sent this lovely piece of mail to me and why. The letter inside looked impressive and very formal, but I couldn't read what it said—it was written in Thai!

Filled with curiosity, I jumped on my bike and rode to my favorite Thai restaurant, where I knew that my friend Chalee, the owner, could translate it for me. "You must know somebody very important!" he said. "This is an official invitation from the king of Thailand to the Royal Plowing Ceremony, a famous event that begins the annual Phraraj Pithi Jarod Phranangkal Reak Na Kwan—the Thai National Celebration of Rice!"

I knew only a little bit about this particular festival, but during my previous travels through Thailand, I was always encountering holidays celebrating rice. One time, having just arrived in Bangkok, the capital of Thailand, I stopped by a bank to exchange my American dollars into the Thai currency, called *baht*. I found a guard standing in front of the padlocked door. "You cannot change money today," he said. "It is a special holiday for the rice harvest."

Another time, when I needed to renew my visa at the embassy in Thailand, an official informed me, "Sorry, no visas available today. We are closed for the rice-planting holiday." And once when I tried to mail a postcard, I saw a sign on the post-office door: "Please come back tomorrow. Today we are sending rockets to the sky to bring rain to our rice fields."

≪ This is the spot where I took my first rice photograph. Surrounded by rivers that provide a full supply of water all year long, this field always has some rice growing—even during the dry season, when the rest of the country has completed the harvest.

≫ The invitation to the Royal Plowing Ceremony came to me embossed in shiny gold and written in a graceful Thai script.

⌃ A pond formed on the edge of a rice paddy is the perfect place for an afternoon swim. Thai children get a holiday at the start of the rainy season.

Eventually, I learned that for the Thai people, their calendar, holidays, and school vacations all reflect the seasons and cycles of rice growing. I tried to imagine a similar set of holidays back in the United States dedicated to wheat or apples or doughnuts, and could not. In Thai culture, however, rice and life are sewn together. So, where better to start learning more about rice than to photograph the event that begins the rice-growing season in Thailand?

Thai farmers begin the planting of rice in late May, before the start of the summer rainy season. But every rice farmer, even those in remote countryside regions, will wait to scatter their seeds until after the Royal Plowing Ceremony. This special event takes place in a Bangkok field near the grand palace of the king.

As the invitation requested, I arrived at six in the morning to join a line of photographers outside the royal palace. I was a bit nervous when I noticed that all the other photographers and TV camera people were wearing dark suits and polished leather shoes. I was dressed in my sturdy traveling photographer clothes—which were great for crawling on the ground for low angle shots but seemed like they might be out of place now.

"Don't you know the rules?" the prim and proper receptionist asked me when she saw me in my old shirt and cargo shorts. "You have to be formally dressed when in the presence of the royal family, and today the crown prince is leading the procession!"

I couldn't believe it. I had traveled all the way to Thailand and now I couldn't go inside because I wasn't wearing a formal suit and necktie!

I rushed back to find my friend Colonel Dewa, who had brought me to the palace. When I explained the situation to him, he chuckled and assured me, "Don't worry. This is Bangkok. We can find anything here."

So we ran to a nearby neighborhood and began knocking on apartment doors and rapping on the shutters of closed clothing stores.

Finally, to my amazement, we found a store filled with dark suits, shoes, and ties all lined up on rack. And best of all, it was even open at six thirty in the morning! I tried on suit after suit until I found one that sort of fit.

With only minutes to spare, I sprinted back to the gate. The same woman whom I had spoken to earlier cried, "Just in the nick of time!" when she saw me running toward her in my newly rented suit.

⩔ Rice farmers from Issan province surround me for a group photo in my rented suit following the Royal Plowing Ceremony.

⌃The Thai minister of agriculture throws out rice seeds during the Royal Plowing Ceremony. He is the head of the ministry that governs all of the crops that are grown in the country. The ministry has been around since the fourteenth century!

I had just enough time to catch my breath and find a spot with good visibility before the ceremony began. First, the minister of agriculture picked up the perfect rice seeds, which were grown within the palace walls, and tossed them out onto the oval dirt track. A shimmering white team of the king's royal oxen followed closely behind him, plowing these extra-special seeds into the ground.

Hundreds of farming families from all over Thailand had traveled through the night to attend this ceremony. As they watched and waited, I could see the flimsy fence in front of them begin to sag and fall over as they pressed forward in anticipation. Once the slow-moving seed-spreading procession rounded the field for the third and final circuit, the fences toppled and people rushed out to collect some of the blessed seeds, just as they and their ancestors did every year.

⌃ After the royal oxen finish plowing the field, they are given seven different dishes to eat from. Their choices predict how those crops will grow in the coming year.

Children dove into the dirt first, carefully sifting and picking out every seed. Their smiles grew larger with each "royal" seed that they uncovered. Within a few minutes, all the seeds had been gathered, and then the dirt itself was scooped up and carefully placed in bags to bring home. Within minutes the "field" was gone and the asphalt below was all that remained.

The farmers and their families beamed with joy because they believe that this royal blessing from their king, Bhumibol Adulyadej, also known as Rama IX, will guarantee a bountiful crop. Once they arrive home, the farmers will sprinkle the prized seeds and sacred dirt onto

《 A farmer's daughter shows off the seeds and soil she has collected. She may plant these with her family's seeds or keep them somewhere special.

△ A Thai farmer walks through a muddy field, tossing rice seeds one handful at a time.

their fields along with thousands of other rice seeds.

After the plowing ceremony, I spent many days in the northeastern part of the country, crisscrossing the flatlands of the Issan region. Famous for the delicate and prized jasmine rice that grows here, Issan is often called the Rice Bowl of Thailand. In Thai, jasmine rice is called *khao suay*, which means "beautiful rice."

The fattest and most nutritious varieties of rice, like jasmine rice, grow best in soft, soggy soil. Walls of dirt cakes surround the sunken fields and form earthen dams that hold the soupy mud inside. This chocolate-colored pool is called a rice paddy. To begin planting, the farmer hand-tosses seeds into the fudgy wet mixture, where they will then take root. Most farmers step into the brown mushy soil wearing thin rubber boots, but children usually just plop in barefoot, sinking slowly into the thick, deep mud. When they pull their feet up, the mud burps at them with a sucking sound and they break into squeals of laughter.

Not much has changed over the centuries in the rice fields of Issan. On thousands of small family plots, farmers have passed down many of the same tools and farming methods for generations. Growing trillions of rice grains requires wide-open fields, lots of sun and rain, hours of hard labor, some crazy-looking machines, and even an elephant or a water buffalo. These powerful animals, often called Asian tractors, help to plow through the thick mud and can carry heavy loads on their backs.

As I walk through the fields, photographing farmers and machines, animals and children—and carrying my huge camera and twenty pounds of backup gear—sweat soaks through my clothing. It seems

⌃ A young elephant and her trainer cross a flooded rice paddy. Elephants are very important in Thailand: they are used in agriculture and for transportation, and are the national symbol of the country.

« A colorful rice-harvesting machine called a combine is unloaded. Each owner paints his or her combine in bold colors and patterns to please the spirits that watch over the fields.

17

⌃ As temperatures rise as high as 100 degrees Fahrenheit, Thai farmers keep every inch of their skin protected from the burning sun.

like I always choose to work in the hottest places on earth. My last adventure was to the equator, in Uganda, which felt very hot at the time, but that was nothing compared to the wet humid air of northeast Thailand! Working outside here is like working inside a steam shower with the door locked and no place to escape to.

I look around me at the Thai farmers who are swaddled in layers and layers of loose silk and cotton—almost every inch of skin covered. With every piece of clothing that I tear off to try to cool myself down, someone smiles at me while pulling her scarf tighter around her shoulders or adding a hat to the top of his head. Even though the Thai farmers look like they might be going out to ski or ice-skate, they are really just protecting themselves from the sun. They also wear hats to help shield their faces from the sun's powerful rays. These hats are called *knob* if they are made out of straw or *muwhack* if they are made from thin strips of bamboo.

≫ Recently transplanted seedlings poke up from a flooded rice field, or paddy. The farmers leave plenty of room around each seedling so it can grow.

Good rains are essential for the rice crop, and Thai farmers look to the spirit world for help to open up the clouds. After the new seeds are planted, the holiday of Bun Bang Fai, "Rocket Days," announces the start of the rainy season. For two full days, farmers parade through town centers, pounding on drums, playing flutes, and singing to the spirits in hopes that they will influence the rainfall. At night they shoot exploding rockets high into the air and blow up noisy firecrackers to awaken the gods who will crack open the clouds.

Once the heavy soaking rains of summer start to fall, the rice seedlings open and their stalks sprout up from the wet ground. Green shoots pop out of the mud like bristles on a hairbrush. When these new bunches have grown to be six

⌃ Rice seedlings are pulled up from a paddy for transplanting.

⌃ After six to eight weeks, seedlings are uprooted and transported quickly to an empty paddy nearby.

inches tall, they will be pulled out by hand and carried to larger fields, where they will have more room to spread out and grow.

One morning, I offer to help a family who is transplanting seedlings. I put down my camera and join them in the paddy, sinking my hands into the warm, thick mud. Although the farmers are all wearing thin cotton gloves, I decide to get my hands dirty and stick my hands right into the soft grit.

When we stop for lunch, I wash and rinse my hands, but I can't get rid of the soil that is stuck under my fingernails and around my knuckles. I scrub harder, but I just can't get the teeny bits of tough earth out from under my nails. Too hungry to care, I decide to forget about my dirty fingernails and plunge into the food.

Unlike in many American households, eating with one's hands is the norm in Thailand. I roll some sticky rice into a ball with my pointer and middle fingers, then use my thumb like a clasp to grab some of the curry. The gooey "sticky rice" of Issan is perfect for soaking up the rich coconut-milk-and-

chili-pepper-based stew we have for lunch. When I finally finish eating, I notice that my hands look sparklingly clean—no more dirt under my nails! Like a sponge, the sticky rice has pulled and scraped off the dirt that had been stuck to my hands.

Once lunch is finished, the farmers go back to work transplanting the seedlings. After each clump is transplanted, one by one, and pushed back into the soft muddy ground, it quickly takes root in its new home.

≫ Children share a snack of warm sticky rice after coming home from school. For Thai people the phrase "to eat" literally means to eat rice—no meal is complete without it.

Over the next few months, it will absorb the heat of the sun and rapidly grow up and up, climbing steadily as it adds one inch per week to its height.

≪ In Thailand, rice is often planted wherever there is open land. Here rice is harvested from a backyard field.

This farmer works from sunrise until late evening hand-cutting each stalk of rice from his field.

In October, each seedling will have become a rice tower crowned with dozens of buds filled with flavor and nutrition. When the rice grains get so heavy that their weight pulls the stalks back down toward the earth, the farmers know it is time to cut them and bring them to the mill. By December, the billions and billions of rice grains will be ready to harvest.

Once the rice is fully grown, farmers must work quickly to cut it down before harsh weather, birds, or mice have a chance to destroy the crop. As harvest time approaches, there is a wave of hustle and bustle as farmers prepare for the weeks of cutting and collecting the rice grains. Parents, grandparents, children, and grandchildren will need to work side by side to harvest the rice together.

≪ This team of family and neighbors will work together to harvest all the rice in their village. Day by day they will move from one field to the next.

Rice growers who can afford to rent shiny, bright combine machines do so, moving from one field to the next. With its cylinders, blades, rods, levers and gears, grinders and pulleys, springs, belts, chutes, and tubes, this giant machine circles through fields, cutting and bagging pound after pound of rice. Other farmers cut the rice fields by hand, using a curved iron sickle called a *kee-oh*.

≪ Birds swoop down to gather rice grass as a combine machine passes over a field. They eat bits of grain that escape the twirling blades and also collect blades of grass to build their nests.

23

⌃Bits of rice grass fly out of a combine machine as rice
buds are mechanically separated from their stalks.

≪ After it is harvested, rice is set out for several days to dry. The farmer will keep a close watch to protect the crop from birds and animals.

The process of separating the fine rice grains from the stalk is called threshing. Once the freshly cut rice has been threshed, farmers set it out to dry in every available open space—front yards, backyards, highways, driveways, fields, or parking lots—wherever they can find a sunny space.

Friends, neighbors, and families all work together to bring in one another's crops. When they finish a hard day of cutting and stacking, they stop and sing together before heading home to a big heaping bowl of rice for supper.

≫ Farmers sing together to celebrate a successful harvest.

Once the rice has dried for a few days, the farmers carry it to the nearby mill for weighing and hulling, a process that peels away the hard brown husk to reveal the fine white rice inside.

After the rice has been hulled, people, machines, and animals fill the roads as farmers carry off scoop after scoop, pile after pile, sack after sack, and truckload after truckload of rice. Tractors that look like motorized broomsticks, dump trucks, carts, and open-air buses overflow with stuffed rice sacks heading to market. Children hop aboard these vehicles for the journey, proudly bouncing up and down on top of

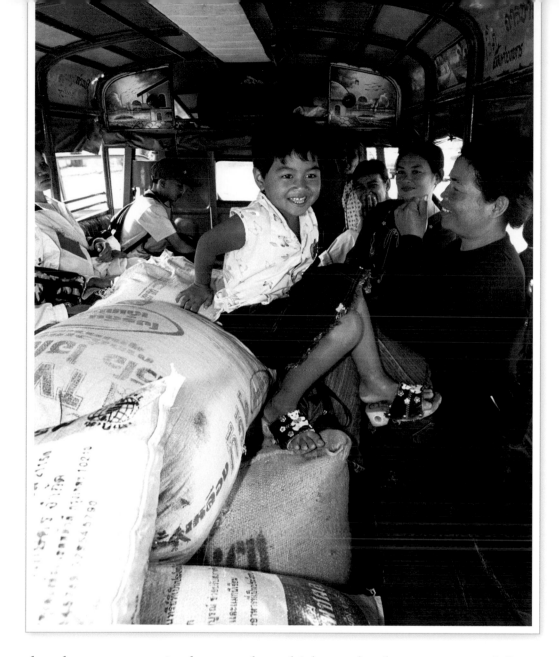

the plump canvas rice bags as thc vchicles make their way to and from the mill. Most of the rice will be sold for a small profit, maybe enough to buy a cow or a motorbike, but a few sacks will be kept at home to feed the farmers' families.

Once the rice grains are removed, the stalks are gathered and piled high. Even this part of the rice plant will have a place in the food chain.

Although the rice buds are the real prizes, no part of the plant goes to waste. One time when I was visiting Thailand in February, a guide told me that all the rice fields would be empty. "Come back in October, when they will be green and full," he said. He was right that the fields were brown, dry, and empty — yet the life of rice hadn't ended. Surrounding the fields were mountains of dry, brown rice stalks. A local farmer explained that none of the rice plant is wasted; the cut rice stalks are used to fertilize gardens or feed cows or are burned as cooking fuel.

⌄Dairy cows have a steady supply of rice stalks to keep them fed.

⌃A rice field is the perfect place for kite flying.

On most days after school is out and the hot tropical sun begins to set, the rice fields become playing fields. The raised dirt tracks are just right for running, racing, and kite flying. The full-grown rice plants are like tiny radiators that hold on to the heat of the day, and as warm wind rises up from the crop, it effortlessly lifts kites high into the air. Children stay out and play until the last light of day fades and their mothers call them home for dinner. A dinner in Thailand will always include their favorite food—rice, of course!

≪ As a group of children run through a flooded rice paddy, they laugh at the squishy sounds of their feet getting stuck in the mud.

The rice cooked in the family kitchen tastes especially sweet to Thai children. For months they watched it grow from tiny seeds to full bouquets of fat yellow buds. Their hands helped plant, bless, nurture, and gather it. If Thai children are asked, *"Khun kin khao rue yung?"* meaning "Are you hungry?" they might say, *"Kin laew kha,"* which means "I have eaten rice today."

≫ As the rice grows, it needs constant attention. This girl helps her family by pulling out weeds.

≪ A water buffalo is guided back to its barn after a day of work plowing the fields.

≫ Sticky rice is kept fresh all day long in straw baskets. In Thailand this is known as Issan style rice.

After I return home from Thailand, each spoonful of rice I eat reminds me of how many hands worked together to grow it. I think of the hot Thai sun that warmed it and the rainy days that watered it. I think of the buffalo pulling the machines and the kids playing with their kites in the field. And I remember all the blessings, from the king and from the spirits, that this rice received in order to make its long journey from a tiny seed to become my supper.

Rice Facts

- Rice is a basic daily food for more than half of the people on earth.

- Rice is grown on every continent except Antarctica.

- More than 600 million tons of rice are grown around the world every year.

- Thailand is the largest exporter of rice to other countries.

- There are over 29,000 individual grains of rice in each pound.

- When it is cooked, rice absorbs water and swells to three times its original weight.

- Rice is a member of the grass family. The two primary cultivated rices are *Oryza sativa* (Asian rice) and *Oryza glaberrima* (African rice).

- Rice is often classified as long-grain, short-grain, or medium-grain, depending on its size and shape. Long-grain is at least three times longer than its width, medium-grain is two to three times longer than its width, and short-grain looks the fattest, as it is only 1½ times as long as its width.

- At least 40,000 different varieties of rice are grown worldwide, although many regional varieties are not marketed or sold outside their local area. Some of the most popular types of rice include:

Basmati rice, from India, Nepal, and Pakistan, has a popcorn-like aroma. Some consider it to be much tastier than white rice, and it is often more expensive.

Sweet rice, also called sticky rice, sticks together as if it were glued. It can be rolled into balls and eaten without utensils.

Arborio rice, from Italy, is fat and puffy and has a creamy texture. It is often used to make risotto.

Jasmine rice, from Thailand, has a delicious aroma and a unique taste. It is considered by many to be the best rice in the world.

Calrose rice, grown in only a few places in the world, has a very mild flavor.

Wild rice is chewy and dark and grows in streams and lakes. Scientifically speaking, it is not considered a true rice. Native Americans have traditionally harvested it from their canoes and roasted it.

Glossary

baht Thai currency

Bangkok the capital of Thailand

Bhumibol Adulyadej also known as Rama IX—king of Thailand

combine machine a tractor with blades, levers, and pulleys. It cuts the rice plants and separates the rice buds from the grass stalks.

Issan province a region in northeastern Thailand famous for the delicate and prized jasmine rice that grows there. Issan is often called the Rice Bowl of Thailand. In Thai, jasmine rice is called *khao suay,* which means "beautiful rice."

hulling a process that peels away the hard brown husk to reveal the white rice inside

kee-oh the curved iron sickle used to cut rice stalks

khao Thai word for rice

Khun kin khao rue yung? *Are you hungry? Literally, Have you eaten rice today?* A traditional Thai greeting.

Kin laew kha *I am not hungry. Literally, I have eaten rice today.*

knob a hat made out of straw

minister of agriculture a high-ranking government official who is in charge of farming and food production

mill a building with special machines to process newly harvested rice and other grains

muwhack a hat made of thin strips of bamboo

rice paddy The word *paddy* comes from the Malaysian language. A paddy is a dug-out field that can hold water when flooded.

threshing the process of separating rice grains from harvested rice stalks

≫ Rice is cut with a *kee-oh.*

⌃ I only had to lean over my balcony at the Four Seasons Resort in Chiang Mai, a city in the north of Thailand, to take this photo of one their gorgeous rice gardens. From every view in the hotel, guests look onto terraced fields reflecting the different growing stages of rice in a mosaic of changing colors. Once the rice is harvested, it is donated to a nearby school for orphaned children.

Rice Holidays

Rice plays an important symbolic role in many Thai religious and regional festivals that celebrate the planting and harvesting seasons. Some of these holidays are nation-wide, while some are celebrated only in specific regions. They are all related to the growing cycle of rice.

APRIL

Songkran · Thai New Year

Thailand's New Year holiday begins in mid-April and lasts for three days. It's called Songkran, a Sanskrit word which means the beginning of a new solar year. Songkran is also a water festival. In Thai culture, water is the symbol of life. An abundance of water will nourish the rice crops that feed the country. Since April is the hottest month of the year, Thai people shower each other with buckets of cold water as a way to cool off and celebrate. The streets become a water park.

Kong Khao · Rice Piling Ceremony

This is an old tradition observed by the people of Chonburi. People in this region of Thailand gather food to offer to the spirits of their ancestors, who protect them throughout the year.

MAY

Phraraj Pithi Jarod Phranangkal Reak Na Kwan · Royal Plowing Ceremony

This ancient ritual celebrates the official start of the rice-growing season. The king or another member of the royal family blesses new rice seeds and tosses them into a large field across from the grand palace in Bangkok. Royal oxen plow the seeds into the soil, which is then collected by farmers and distributed throughout Thailand.

Bun Bang Fai · "Rocket Days" Rainmaking Festival

During this two-day festival, traditionally believed to ensure plentiful rains during the early rice-growing season, villagers in northeastern Thailand hold parades, launch exploding rockets, and set off firecrackers.

AUGUST/SEPTEMBER

Yehkuja · Akha Swing Festival

For four days in late August or early September, when the rice has matured but is not ready to be harvested, the Akha hill tribe in Chiang Rai celebrates with a dance and song festival. This is a time of thanksgiving and a show of respect to their ancestors.

FEBRUARY

Chainat "Hoon Fang" · Straw-Bird Festival

Straw is a plentiful by-product in rice farming, and the villagers of Chainat, in central Thailand, use it to create colorful straw birds representing the more than eighty-five species that are found in the Chainat Bird Park. The straw birds are displayed in a town fair that also features a variety of delicious preparations of rice.

Some Thai Rice Dishes

khao neow sticky rice

khao neow mumwang sticky rice with mango

khao pad fried rice

khao plow jasmine rice

khao poon rice noodles

khao suay steamed jasmine rice

khao tom rice soup

>> **A woman is hidden behind the tall rice buds ready for harvest.**